INSIGHT FOR L

W9-CKC-487

Broadcast Schedule

Songs for All Seasons

January 29–February 15, 2001

Monday	**January 29**	**The Significance of Songs** *Selected Scriptures*
Tuesday	**January 30**	**The Significance of Songs**
Wednesday	**January 31**	**A Song of Single-Mindedness** *Psalm 1*
Thursday	**February 1**	**A Song of Single-Mindedness**
Friday	**February 2**	**A Song for Times of Crisis** *Psalm 13*

Monday	**February 5**	**A Song for Times of Crisis**
Tuesday	**February 6**	**A Song of Sovereignty** *Psalm 46*
Wednesday	**February 7**	**A Song of Sovereignty**
Thursday	**February 8**	**A Song of Sovereignty**
Friday	**February 9**	**Two Songs for Moms and Dads** *Psalms 127–128*

Monday	**February 12**	**Two Songs for Moms and Dads**
Tuesday	**February 13**	**A Song of Reassurance** *Psalm 139*
Wednesday	**February 14**	**A Song of Reassurance**
Thursday	**February 15**	**A Song of Reassurance**

Broadcast schedule is subject to change without notice.

Insight for Living • Post Office Box 69000, Anaheim, CA 92817-0900
Insight for Living Ministries • Post Office Box 2510, Vancouver, BC, Canada V6B 3W7
Insight for Living, Inc. • 20 Albert Street, Blackburn, VIC 3130, Australia
Printed in the United States of America

SONGS
for All
SEASONS

From the Bible-Teaching Ministry of

Charles R. Swindoll

INSIGHT FOR LIVING

Charles R. Swindoll graduated in 1963 from Dallas Theological Seminary, where he now serves as the school's fourth president, helping to prepare a new generation of men and women for the ministry. Chuck has served in pastorates in three states: Massachusetts, Texas, and California, including almost twenty-three years at the First Evangelical Free Church in Fullerton, California. He is currently senior pastor of Stonebriar Community Church in Frisco, Texas, north of Dallas. His sermon messages have been aired over radio since 1979 as the *Insight for Living* broadcast. A best-selling author, he has written numerous books and booklets on many subjects.

Based on the outlines, charts, and transcripts of Charles R. Swindoll's sermons, the study guide text was developed and written by the Pastoral Ministries Department at Insight for Living.

Editor in Chief:
Cynthia Swindoll

Study Guide Writer:
Mark Tobey

Senior Editor and Assistant Writer:
Wendy Peterson

Editors:
Karla Lenderink
Christianne Varvel

Rights and Permissions:
The Meredith Agency

Text Designer:
Gary Lett

Graphic System Administrator:
Bob Haskins

Director, Communications Division:
John Norton

Print Production Manager:
Don Bernstein

Printer:
Sinclair Printing Company

Unless otherwise identified, all Scripture references are from the New American Standard Bible, updated edition, copyright © The Lockman Foundation 1960, 1962, 1963, 1968, 1971, 1972, 1973, 1975, 1977, 1995. Used by permission. Scripture taken from the Holy Bible, New International Version, Copyright © 1973, 1978, 1984 International Bible Society, used by permission of Zondervan Bible Publishers [NIV].

Psalms/Now by Leslie Brandt. Copyright © 1996 by Concordia Publishing House. Used with permission under license number 00:9–121.

An effort has been made to locate sources and obtain permission where necessary for the quotations used in this book. In the event of any unintentional omission, a modification will gladly be incorporated in future printings.

ISBN 1-57972-358-6

Cover design: Lauriana Fortuna

Cover images: © 2000 (Timothy Shonnard)/Stone

Printed in the United States of America

CONTENTS

1   The Significance of Songs   1
        Selected Scriptures

2   A Song of Single-Mindedness   8
        Psalm 1

3   A Song for Times of Crisis   17
        Psalm 13

4   A Song of Sovereignty   25
        Psalm 46

5   Two Songs for Moms and Dads   33
        Psalms 127–128

6   A Song of Reassurance   42
        Psalm 139

    Books for Probing Further   53

    Notes   55

    Ordering Information   59

INTRODUCTION

I love to sing. In fact, I love to sing *loudly*. I have wonderful memories of my brother and sister and me standing around the family piano singing songs and hymns . . . one after another . . . at the top of our lungs. It's amazing how those grand theological truths woven through each stanza took up permanent residence in my mind and heart.

Though I love them all, I suppose I do have my favorites, like "Immortal Invisible, God Only Wise," "My Hope Is in the Lord," "Come, Thou Fount of Every Blessing," "And Can It Be?" and of course, "All Hail the Power of Jesus' Name"! Even today, I keep a dog-eared hymnal near my desk for easy reference. In my times with the Lord, I often turn to one of those old standbys and allow the familiar strains to fill my heart again.

But there is another hymnal that's close to my heart—an ancient Songbook that tells of a people and their God in a time now past. It tells of their struggles. Their victories. Their pain. Their celebrations. I'm talking, of course, about the Psalms—150 of the most remarkable expressions of human experience ever penned. And I love all of them. Still, like the hymns, I do have a few favorites.

In this study, we will look at six psalms that have been a continual source of encouragement to me over the years. I hope that when we've completed our time together in the Psalms, you will have gained not only a deeper appreciation for these rich songs of wisdom and truth but, more importantly, a closer walk with the Lord, who speaks through them.

Chuck Swindoll

Charles R. Swindoll

PUTTING TRUTH
INTO ACTION

K nowledge apart from application falls short of God's desire for His children. He wants us to apply what we learn so that we will change and grow. This study guide was prepared with these goals in mind. As you go through the following pages, we hope your desire to discover biblical truth will grow as your understanding of God's Word increases, and that you will be encouraged to apply what you've learned.

To assist you in your study, we've included a section called Living Insights at the end of each lesson. These exercises will challenge you to study further and to think of specific ways to put your discoveries into action.

There are many ways to use this guide—in personal devotions, group studies, discussions with friends and family, and Sunday school classes. And, of course, it's an ideal study aid when you're listening to its corresponding *Insight for Living* radio series.

To benefit most from this study guide, we would encourage you to consider it a spiritual journal. That's why we've included space in the **Living Insights** for recording your thoughts and discoveries. We hope you'll return to those sections often for review and en-couragement as you continue to grow in your walk with Christ.

Insight for Living

SONGS
for All
SEASONS

Chapter 1

THE SIGNIFICANCE OF SONGS
Selected Scriptures

In the beginning God created the foundations of the earth, and

> the morning stars sang together
> And all the sons of God shouted for joy. (Job 38:7)

And it was very good!

Author Mike Mason notes, "Scientists today like to talk about the Big Bang; but little do they realize that the echoes they detect may be shouts of angels."[1]

Long before Adam drew his first breath, the angelic hosts assembled in song and praise for the Creator of heaven and earth. And long after this earth passes away and God ushers in His new creation, all heaven will still be singing—singing a new song to the Savior of the world:

> "Worthy are You to take the book and to break its seals; for You were slain, and purchased for God with Your blood men from every tribe and tongue and people and nation. You have made them to be a kingdom and priests to our God; and they will reign upon the earth."
>
>   . . . "Worthy is the Lamb that was slain to receive power and riches and wisdom and might and honor and glory and blessing." (Rev. 5:9b–10, 12b)

---

1. Mike Mason, *The Gospel According to Job* (Wheaton, Ill.: Good News Publishers, Crossway Books, 1994), p. 392.

"The secret of the universe is a shout of joy," Mason tells us, and "ecstasy is the cornerstone and foundation of absolutely everything."[2]

From beginning to end, creation to re-creation, music fills God's story. The Bible is replete with salvation's songs, showing us that the Lord's people are a singing people. The instinct of faith is to sing, and God's people have long shared their faith, privately and corporately, through song.

Now, some of you who, at your best, can only manage a "joyful noise" may be worried that we're going to urge you into the church choir—or worse, the Sunday solo. Relax! Many of us do our best singing to the Lord in our hearts. But that doesn't mean we have nothing to gain from the singing and songs of others.

For the next little while, you are invited to take a front-row, center seat and to trace the melodies of faith God has recorded from beginning to end in His Word. Then we'll raise the curtain on the richest trove of songs in the Bible—the book of Psalms.

So take your seat. The houselights are dimming, the conductor has raised his baton, and the overture is about to begin.

A Survey of Songs in the Bible

With the introduction of Jubal (Gen. 4:21), the ancient father of musicians, a line of musical tradition commenced that runs throughout the Scriptures. The first to play string and wind instruments, Jubal passed along his talent to all music makers to come. In Israel's history alone, a professional association of worship musicians was well established by the time Israel was worshiping in the tabernacle.[3]

Old Testament Songs of Praise

From Genesis, we travel to Exodus 15 and hear echoes of an ancient song of gratitude for the Lord's deliverance of Israel from Pharaoh's army (vv. 1–21). Led by Moses and his sister Miriam, this is the first song recorded in the Bible. Later, in the book of Judges, Deborah and Barak sang a song of praise to the Lord for His intervention on behalf of Israel against the Canaanites (Judg. 5).

---

2. Mason, *The Gospel According to Job*, p. 391.

3. Donald P. Hustad, *Jubilate! Church Music in the Evangelical Tradition* (Carol Stream, Ill.: Hope Publishing Co., 1981), p. 81.

But the glory days of Hebrew song did not begin until David picked up his harp. From his days as a shepherd tending his father's flock to his reign as king over Israel, David composed a body of hymns that make up the bulk of Israel's hymnbook, the Psalms. After him, Solomon assumed not only his father's role as king of Israel, but also his role as chief songwriter for Jewish temple worship. Solomon alone composed over one thousand songs (1 Kings 4:32)!

Of course, not all the singing was joyful. Israel experienced great hardship, centuries of bondage, and years of backbreaking judgment. Many of these songs were composed in minor keys, reflecting the pain and disillusionment of a people prone to wander.

Psalm 137 is such a song, borne out of the duress of exile. Haunted by memories of humiliation and suffering, deep regret filled the people's hearts as they sang of the biting sarcasm of their captors:[4]

> For there our captors demanded of us songs,
> And our tormentors mirth, saying,
> "Sing us one of the songs of Zion." (Ps. 137:3)

The Old Testament ends with a warning of judgment (Mal. 1–4) and a deafening silence from heaven. As the scene closes, the mood is dark, and the familiar strains of faith and hope are replaced with silence and shadows.

The Gospel Song of Salvation

Thankfully, into this great darkness came an even greater Light! As the curtain rises once again on Israel, the strains become melodic, filled with hope and joy. The New Testament opens with exuberant singing at the advent of the Messiah.

The first singer is an unlikely one, plucked from obscurity by an angelic messenger with an oracle from heaven.

> Now in the sixth month the angel Gabriel was sent from God to a city in Galilee called Nazareth, to a virgin engaged to a man whose name was Joseph, of the descendants of David; and the virgin's name was Mary. And coming in, he said to her, . . .

---

4. Some commentators believe that up to two-thirds of the Psalms were composed during the post-exilic period, that is, in the years following the Babylonian captivity (for example, Psalms 102, 126, and 137). A more conservative estimate is one-third. Current scholarly consensus holds that composition of the Psalms ranges from the time of the Exodus to after the Exile.

"Behold, you will conceive in your womb and bear a son, and you shall name Him Jesus. He will be great and will be called the Son of the Most High; and the Lord God will give Him the throne of His father David." (Luke 1:26–28a, 31–32)

Heartened by the angel's announcement, Mary sang a song of praise to the Lord (vv. 46–55) that began with these words:

"My soul exalts the Lord,
And my spirit has rejoiced in God my Savior.
For He has had regard for the humble state of His
    bondslave;
For behold, from this time on all generations will
    count me blessed." (vv. 46b–48)

And just as angels sang at the birth of the world, angels joined in chorus to announce the new birth that would be ushered into the world with the coming of the Messiah:

"Glory to God in the highest,
And on earth peace among men with whom He is
    pleased." (Luke 2:14)

The joyful song is back!

Jesus called His disciples and built into them the words of life they would one day proclaim to the far corners of the world. Then, as He drew near to the cross, Jesus invited His disciples to join Him for a very special meal, in which He shared with them the events that were to come.

While they were eating, Jesus took some bread, and after a blessing, He broke it and gave it to the disciples, and said, "Take, eat; this is My body." And when He had taken a cup and given thanks, He gave it to them, saying, "Drink from it, all of you; for this is My blood of the covenant, which is poured out for many for forgiveness of sins." (Matt. 26:26–28)

Matthew then notes an interesting detail: "After singing a hymn, they went out to the Mount of Olives" (v. 30). So the disciples joined in singing with Jesus as He prepared for His death on the cross.

New Testament Songs of Praise

The early church was a singing church. Luke told us that Paul and Silas even sang hymns while in jail in Philippi (Acts 16:25). Throughout his epistles, Paul urged believers to encourage "one another in psalms and hymns and spiritual songs" (Eph. 5:19; Col. 3:16). And the New Testament closes with the book of Revelation providing a stirring finale of praise to a risen and reigning Christ!

> "To him who sits on the throne, and to the Lamb,
> be blessing and honor and glory and dominion forever and ever." (Rev. 5:13b)

Lingering Lessons

God's revelation begins and ends with a song. And we are encouraged to sing of Him and His marvelous grace, not only to each other, but to the people of the world. You cannot read the Bible without developing a profound appreciation for the gift of song to the experience of faith.

Three principles emerge for us to consider before we embark on our study of six favorite psalms. First, *since the beginning, songs have been present and blessed by God. The challenge? Remain sensitive to them*. Worship is not simply an act of the spirit but also of the mind. We must pay attention to the words and think about what they mean, not just float away on a cloud of emotion (see 1 Cor. 14:15). So be sensitive to what you are singing.

Second, *the purpose of singing has always been wide and varied. The challenge? Broaden your taste*. Worship music in the church has undergone sweeping changes in recent decades. Differing styles and forms exist in abundance. Many are tempted to resist change and maintain an attitude of inflexibility with regard to music in the church, but God would have us resist that temptation and remain open to His Spirit. Remember: the great old hymns of today were once the new worship songs of the past!

And last, *God reserved His longest book in the Bible for songs. The challenge? Be a good student of the Songbook*. No other book in the Bible has as many chapters as the book of Psalms. It would be a worthy discipline to commit several psalms or portions of them to memory each year. Plant the words of these magnificent poems deep within your heart.

And remember, songs were meant to be sung. So go ahead! Sing them with all your heart!

 *Living Insights*

What is *your* song? What do you sing today? Perhaps yours is a song of discouragement, even fear, as you wrestle with the loss of a loved one.

Maybe it's a song of worry. Life's loose ends have wrapped themselves around your neck, choking your ability to sing. Too much to do, too little time to do it all. Maybe you've lost your job and the comfortable feelings of security you once enjoyed are slipping away with each passing week.

Or perhaps you've stopped singing completely. Circumstances have you so paralyzed that you've begun to grow numb to the voice of God.

Are you harboring sin? Are those stubborn patterns of disobedience, long fought but never broken, robbing you of any shred of joy or peace?

What song are you singing today? How would you describe it?

_____

_____

_____

_____

Here is great news for you: No matter where you are or what song you sing, the Lord specializes in putting new songs in our hearts!

Take some time to read Psalm 40 and meditate on its words of praise. The psalmist took comfort in the fact that, no matter how low his spirits had dropped, God was able to lift him out of the gloom and cause him to sing again. Write down some of the other reasons the psalmist had to praise God.

_____

_____

_____

_____

_____

_____

_____

_____

Over the next few weeks, reacquaint yourself with the Song-book. Leaf through its pages; some of them, no doubt, are well worn, while others are clearly untouched. Read a few out loud and others quietly to yourself. Write down or underline the words that bring special comfort and encouragement to you. And as you do, ask the Lord to meet you in the Psalms . . . to bring you fresh perspective . . . to tune your heart to *His* song. Soon you'll feel a new song beginning to emerge.

Happy singing!

Chapter 2

A SONG OF SINGLE-MINDEDNESS
Psalm 1

As we open the Lord's Songbook, a wonderful word greets us: *blessed*. "How blessed is the man" begins the lyric in Psalm 1 —and not only does it start the psalm, but it also welcomes us into the entire book of Psalms. This gateway psalm is here, explains Hebrew scholar James Mays, "to invite us to read and use the entire book as a guide to a blessed life."[1] And James Montgomery Boice adds that beginning the book with a blessing

> is important certainly, for it is a way of saying that
> the psalms (as well as all Scripture) have been given
> to us by God to do us good.[2]

The good that God pronounces in Psalm 1, however, is not given indiscriminately; it is bestowed on those who choose a particular direction for their lives. In a fine paraphrase, Leslie Brandt captures the heart of this psalm's message:

> Those persons who choose to live significant lives
>   are not going to take their cues
>   from the religiously indifferent.
> Nor will they conform to the crowd
>   nor mouth their prejudices
>   nor dote on the failures of others.
>
> Their ultimate concern is the will of God.
> They make their daily decisions in respect to such.
> Compare them to a sturdy tree
>   planted in rich, moist soil.

1. James Luther Mays, *Psalms*, Interpretation: A Bible Commentary for Teaching and Preaching Series (Louisville, Ky.: John Knox Press, 1994), p. 40.

2. James Montgomery Boice, *Psalms: An Expositional Commentary* (Volume 1, Psalms 1–41) (Grand Rapids, Mich.: Baker Book House, 1994), p. 15. The first note in the melody of the Psalms sounds the Lord's blessing, and the final note offers praise to the Giver of blessings (Ps. 150).

As the tree yields fruit,
>   so their lives manifest blessing for others
>   and are purposeful and productive.

This is not true concerning the ungodly.
They are like sand in a desert storm
>   or leaves in an autumn wind.
They cannot stand against the judgments
>   of the eternal God.
And they are most uncomfortable
>   among those who demonstrate genuine faith
>   in the God of righteousness.

The children of God walk in the course
>   that God has ordained.
The children of unbelief walk
>   in paths of self-destruction.[3]

With the overarching theme of this song lingering in our thoughts, let's now tune our minds to the message of each stanza.

The Godly Life Explained

As we journey into this wisdom psalm, we discover that it contrasts two groups of people: the godly (blessed) and the ungodly (wicked). What distinguishes the one from the other?

The *godly*, according to Scripture—and particularly the Psalms—are those individuals who are in a right relationship with God through faith. They have made an unswerving commitment to obey God's revealed instruction in His Word. The godly love the Lord and His ways, and they keep Him at the center of their lives.

The *ungodly*, or "wicked," on the other hand, reject the Lord and His righteous decrees, setting themselves on a path marked by disobedience. They have no regard for God's standards of living. Essentially, ungodliness is living as if God did not exist at all.

Psalm 1 says much about the end results of both ways of living—because the choices we make today inevitably come to bear on the quality of life tomorrow. Through a series of contrasts, the psalmist laid plain the ways of the godly and the wicked and the destiny of both.

3. Leslie F. Brandt, *Psalms Now*, rev. ed. (St. Louis, Mo.: Concordia Publishing House, 1996), p. 15. Psalm 1 falls into the category of "wisdom psalms," which are psalms that explain truth for living in right relationship with God and those around us.

Godly People Are Blessed

The psalmist began by explaining that the godly are blessed *for what they don't do.*

> How blessed is the man who does not walk in the
>   counsel of the wicked,
> Nor stand in the path of sinners,
> Nor sit in the seat of scoffers! (Ps. 1:1)

What exactly does *blessed* mean? The Hebrew word, *esher,* "is actually a plural, which denotes either a multiplicity of blessings or an intensification of them"[4]—we could render it "happinesses" or "bliss." The word implies a sense of remarkable well-being that would be enviously desired: "To be envied with desire is the man who trusts in the Lord."[5] It also includes the idea of "spiritual peace and joy that results from" a right relationship with God.[6] For the psalmist, a blessed life is a life of genuine meaning and fulfillment.

How do people become blessed? By *not* doing three things:

1. They don't walk in the counsel of the wicked.

2. They don't stand in the path of sinners.

3. They don't sit in the seat of scoffers.

In these three lines, the psalmist used a form of parallelism that intensifies the level of involvement with the ungodly. The movement from walking to standing to sitting suggests an insidious progression downward—from being casually influenced by the ungodly to fully colluding with them.

As the world around us darkens, growing increasingly hostile to truth, morality, honesty, and character, we need to decide how we'll respond to it. Sometimes we're tempted to compromise—to slip quietly into the crowd by slowly adjusting our expectations and standards to the culture's. But once we've accepted this "accommodation theology," softening and blurring the clear mandates of God's

---

4. Boice, *Psalms (Volume 1, Psalms 1–41),* p. 15.

5. R. Laird Harris, Gleason L. Archer Jr., and Bruce K. Waltke, eds., *Theological Wordbook of the Old Testament* (Chicago, Ill.: Moody Press, 1980), vol. 1, p. 80.

6. Allen P. Ross, "Psalms," in *The Bible Knowledge Commentary,* Old Testament edition, ed. John F. Walvoord and Roy B. Zuck (Colorado Springs, Colo.: Chariot Victor Publishing, 1985), p. 790.

Word in order to "get along," we slide downhill fast into collusion with evil. Accommodation leads away from godliness and lands us far from lasting happiness.

As the godly are blessed for *not* following the ways outlined in verse 1, they are also blessed *for* following the course described in verse 2.

The Godly Delight in God's Word

The psalmist next emphasized two elements of the godly life:

> But his delight is in the law of the Lord,
> And in His law he meditates day and night. (v. 2)

First, the godly delight "in the law of the Lord"—which is generally understood to be God's will or instruction as revealed in His Word.[7] What is it about God's Word that brings delight and blessing?

- It provides necessary absolutes in a world without them.

- It gives a meaningful view of life in a world that's futile, empty, and filled with cynicism.

- It tells us the truth in a world that's awash in lies and uncertainties.

In this first part of verse 2, then, the psalmist was emphasizing that the Lord blesses the individual who grows to more deeply appreciate both the temporal and eternal values of submitting to God's Word.

Second, the godly and blessed person "meditates day and night" on the truths of God's Word. This is practical instruction that encourages us to flood our minds with the living words of Scripture. We do this through reading, studying, memorizing, and applying God's Word. We take its challenges to heart, and we find peace in its promises. This is what Paul was talking about when he spoke of being transformed by the renewing of our minds (Rom. 12:2)—we become different people when we let God's Word permeate our minds and hearts.

What are the results of delighting in and meditating on God's Word? The psalmist described them in verse 3.

---

7. See Walter Brueggemann, *The Message of the Psalms: A Theological Commentary* (Minneapolis, Minn.: Augsburg Publishing House, 1984), pp. 38–39.

The Godly Are "Like a Tree Firmly Planted"

Invoking one of the most vivid word pictures in all of Scripture, the psalmist revealed that the godly person

> will be like a tree firmly planted by streams of water,
> Which yields its fruit in its season
> And its leaf does not wither;
> And in whatever he does, he prospers. (Ps. 1:3)

The godly life is likened to a flourishing tree, a common metaphor in Scripture (see Prov. 11:30; 15:4; Jer. 17:7–8; Ezek. 47:12). The godly person's roots are "firmly planted"—stable and strong, able to withstand life's storms. The godly life is "planted" near running water—continually receiving rich nourishment from the Scriptures. And it is blanketed with abundant foliage and fruit in its season—prospering with a fulfilling, meaningful life. Not necessarily great wealth, but God's richest blessing on all of life!

Psalm 92 provides a parallel image of the blessed life of the godly:

> The righteous man will flourish like the palm tree,
> He will grow like a cedar in Lebanon.
> Planted in the house of the Lord,
> They will flourish in the courts of our God.
> They will still yield fruit in old age;
> They shall be full of sap and very green. (vv. 12–14)

Even in old age, the godly person who has invested his or her life in what is eternal will still be bearing fruit for God!

The ungodly, or "wicked," however, have something else in store.

The Ungodly Life Explained

Here the psalm inevitably turns solemn as the psalmist painted a grim portrait of the life lived apart from God.

The Ungodly Are Not Like the Blessed

Verse 4 literally begins: "Not so the wicked." All that the psalmist had previously described in terms of blessing and prosperity for the righteous is not true for the wicked. They will not be happy many times over; they are not directed in the ways of truth; and they will not become as the firmly planted tree—stable, nourished, and fruitful.

Rather, the wicked will be like the wind-driven chaff—insubstantial, useless.

The Ungodly Are Like Chaff

But they are like chaff which the wind drives away.
(v. 4b)

Just the sound of it is bleak, isn't it? *Chaff*. The word is abrasive. Transient. Abrupt. So like the life it represents. Here one day and—at the slightest breeze—gone the next. Pastor Ray Stedman gives us a firsthand description of what chaff is like.

> I do not think city folks understand chaff. In Montana every fall we had harvesters who came around with a thrashing rig. The bundles of wheat would be thrown into this machine. The straw would be blown out onto the stack and the wheat would come dribbling out to be poured into trucks or wagons and taken away to the granary. But floating around in the air everywhere was chaff. It was the "awfullest stuff" you ever saw. It stuck to the skin wherever you were sweating—on the back of your neck and down your shirt. It created frightful itching. It was universally regarded as totally worthless.
>   . . . The only thing they could think of to do with chaff was to let the wind blow it away.[8]

That's the true nature of the ungodly life. No roots. No value. No lasting contribution. The godly enjoy meaning and fulfillment—deep roots, rich fruit. But not so the wicked. They are blown away like dust.

The ungodly don't always look that unstable on the surface, though, do they? Many live well. Often, they represent the main-stream of wealth and influence in society. They drive the expensive cars, live in the luxury homes, and travel all over the world, while many godly believers do their best to simply pile the family in the old car and get to church on time!

What gives?

A glance at the eternal time frame might help answer that.

---

8. Ray C. Stedman, *Psalms of Faith: A Life-Related Study from Selected Psalms*, rev. ed. (Ventura, Calif.: Gospel Light Publications, Regal Books, 1988), p. 20. Derek Kidner adds that chaff is "the ultimate in what is rootless, weightless" and is linked to what the KJV calls "vain and light persons" (Judg. 9:4). *Psalms 1–72: An Introduction and Commentary on Books I and II of the Psalms*, The Tyndale Old Testament Commentaries Series (Downers Grove, Ill.: InterVarsity Press, 1973), p. 49.

The Ungodly Have a Frightful Destiny

The ungodly may have some material success, but they won't experience genuine, lasting fulfillment. And those who turn their backs on God will ultimately be found wanting in the life hereafter. Notice the transition in verse 5:

> Therefore the wicked will not stand in the judgment,
> Nor sinners in the assembly of the righteous.

The psalmist predicted certain peril for unbelievers when they come before the holy God. Unlike the righteous, who will stand tall in the grace of Jesus Christ, the wicked will bow in shame to receive their just and eternal sentence. As commentator Walter Brueggemann notes, "The connection between devotion and destiny is not negotiable."[9] Their temporal prosperity does not mean that they are exempt from judgment here on earth; their judgment has simply been deferred to the future.

The last verse of Psalm 1 gives us our final contrast:

> For the Lord knows the way of the righteous,
> But the way of the wicked will perish. (v. 6)

The psalmist uses the most intimate of words to describe the relationship between the Lord and the righteous: He *knows* their way. In other words, the Lord's primary concern is for the ultimate well-being of the righteous.

In contrast, "the way of the wicked will perish." A day is coming when all people will stand before the Lord as Judge. He who knows us from the inside out, who discerns the motives behind our actions, and who knows truth from error will judge the godly and the ungodly. The godly will be blessed. The ungodly will be unable to stand. Those who have chosen to live their lives apart from God's goodness will perish—separation from God without parole.

"The way of the wicked *will* perish." The deathly judgment of the wicked is no less certain than the blessedness of the godly. Two ways to live. Two destinies. Both sure.

So, which way will you choose? In Moses' last words to the Israelites, he could have been speaking of this psalm: "I have set before you life and death, the blessing and the curse. So choose life . . ." (Deut. 30:19). God wants you to choose Him, because

---

9. Brueggemann, *The Message of the Psalms*, p. 39.

in Him are blessing, delight, meaning, and life! In His presence there is "fullness of joy," and in His outstretched hand "there are pleasures forever" (Ps. 16:11). So choose the way of the blessed, won't you? It's the path blazed by the God who wants to do you good!

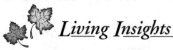 *Living Insights*

What is the message of Psalm 1 in a nutshell? How about this: *Multiplied happiness comes from being single-mindedly committed to the Lord.*

Genuine happiness comes from wise, God-centered living— especially in a day when God's wisdom is publicly scorned.

Perhaps you have been on a lifelong search for true happiness. Or maybe you are searching for happiness lost—a happiness you thought you possessed until it left along with your marriage, your children, or your health.

None of those things, as wonderful as they can be, bring lasting, genuine happiness. What does is a life lived according to God's plan as revealed in His Word. The psalmist says to look no further than the pages of the Bible for the key to a blessed life! Following God's plan is a positive, fulfilling way to live—a way that leads to happiness, whatever the circumstances.

Try this. Read through Psalm 1 again. As you do, circle the characteristics of the godly and the ungodly. Then take some time to formulate them in your own words and write them down.

The Godly	The Ungodly

What do you think the psalmist meant by "delighting" in the law of the Lord?

_____

_____

_____

_____

_____

_____

What are some ways in which you can delight in the Lord?

_____

_____

_____

_____

_____

_____

Now, take some time to pray. Ask the Lord to help you examine your priorities—those areas of your life that mean the most to you. Ask the Holy Spirit to point out attitudes, actions, or feelings that do not honor the Lord. As He does, confess them and ask the Lord for forgiveness.

Finally, make a commitment to begin meditating on a certain portion of Scripture each day. Perhaps a good time would be when you are preparing to sleep at night. A better time may be when you are folding laundry or walking your dog. Find a time when you can clear your mind and focus on the Word of God. It might be a good idea to start with Psalm 1.

Stand by for the blessing!

Chapter 3

A SONG FOR TIMES OF CRISIS
Psalm 13

W ho hasn't felt alone and abandoned? Who can't remember times when God seemed far away? Who doesn't understand when a friend or family member suffers physically or emotionally? Who hasn't asked, "O Lord, how long?"

If those four questions strike a note of relevance, you'll have no difficulty identifying with David's feelings as he composed Psalm 13. Appropriately identified by students of the Psalms as "a psalm of lament," it was conceived in a womb of woe. But, as we shall see, all was not lost. The psalmist may have begun on his face, but he wound up on his feet.

Let's find out what made the difference.

The Background: Why the Lament?

Though David, the composer of this psalm, was a man after God's own heart (1 Sam. 13:14; Acts 13:22), he was no stranger to adversity. In fact, some of his most heartfelt songs flowed from crises.

Psalm 13 may have been composed when David was a fugitive in the Judean desert. Relentless in his pursuit of the young king-to-be, King Saul drove himself mad in his obsession to rid David from his kingdom. So David was on the run. With only crags and caves for shelter, days turned into weeks . . . weeks into months . . . and months into years. Perhaps David's patience with God's timing was running thin.

Or perhaps David was fighting for his life against a grave illness and was not getting any better. The apparent silence of the Lord forced him to cry out in anguish as he questioned God's presence and protection. David's death would mean victory for his enemies and shame for the name of his God.

The fact is, we simply do not know the setting for the psalm. What we do know is that the situation was dire, and from David's perspective, it warranted desperate measures. His only hope was a frantic plea for mercy. This psalm, then, is more a prayer for help than a lament of life's seemingly downward turn. And though

Psalm 13 falls into the general category of a lament, the appeal is for immediate rescue.

The Experience: How Does David Respond?

Leslie Brandt, in *Psalms Now,* captures the emotional intensity of David's prayer in the following paraphrase:

> O God, sometimes You seem so far away.
> I cannot in this moment sense Your presence
>   or feel Your power.
>
> The darkness enveloping me is stifling.
> This depression is suffocating.
> How long, O God, do I have to live in this void?
> O God, how long?
>
> Break into this black night, O God;
>   fill in this vast emptiness.
> Enter into my conflict
>   lest I fall, never to rise again.
>
> I continue to trust in Your ever-present love.
> I shall again discover true joy
>   in my relationship with You.
> I will proclaim Your praises, my Lord,
>   for You will never let me go.[1]

The Predicament

In typical lament form, David began by addressing the Lord directly and, in no uncertain terms, made his complaint plain. He did so with four consecutive questions held together with the repeated phrase "How long?"

> How long, O Lord? Will You forget me forever?
> How long will You hide Your face from me?
> How long shall I take counsel in my soul,
> Having sorrow in my heart all the day?
> How long will my enemy be exalted over me?
> (vv. 1–2)

1. Leslie F. Brandt, *Psalms Now,* rev. ed. (Saint Louis, Mo.: Concordia Publishing House, 1996), p. 29.

The first feeling David expressed was that God had forgotten him. How could God forget one of His servants? He can't, of course, but it felt that way to David. Despair had set in, and David questioned God's concern for his situation. He was feeling utterly abandoned.

He next wondered if God had rejected him—"How long will You hide Your face from me?" (v. 1b). The hiding of a face usually suggests a deliberate sense of distance between two parties, the turning of one's back on another. Essentially, David felt alienated from the Lord. He no longer sensed His presence, His power, or His care. To not see the Lord's face is to not know His blessing, and David wondered what had become of the blessings of mercy, protection, and grace promised by the Lord.[2] Completely disoriented by his circumstances, David felt as though the Lord had not only forgotten him but was deliberately hiding from him.

The third feeling David expressed was deep inner turmoil. By this time, David's perspective was so skewed by the severity of his circumstances that his mind and emotions had shifted into overdrive. He had begun a period of futile, negative musings that had turned his reflections inward. Commentator James Montgomery Boice explains what happens when we enter such a brooding time:

> When we no longer sense that God is blessing us,
> we tend to ruminate on our failures and get into an
> emotional funk. And when our emotions take over
> it is always hard to get back onto a level course.
> This is because the best means of doing this—calm
> reflection and a review of past blessings—are being
> swept away. We discover that we cannot settle our-
> selves long enough to complete the exercise.[3]

Unsettled and weary, David had sunk into a depression. And no relief from the Lord seemed soon in coming.

And, as if David's trouble with God and himself weren't enough, we discover he had trouble with an enemy. We are not told the nature of the menace, but for David the threat was real: "How long will my enemy be exalted over me?" (v. 2b).

---

2. See Willem A. VanGemeren, "Psalms," in *The Expositor's Bible Commentary*, gen. ed. Frank E. Gaebelein (Grand Rapids, Mich.: Zondervan Publishing House, 1991), vol. 5, p. 140.

3. James Montgomery Boice, *Psalms: An Expositional Commentary* (Volume 1, Psalms 1–41) (Grand Rapids, Mich.: Baker Book House, 1994), p. 109.

This final "How long?" may reveal some resentment David might have harbored toward God for allowing his enemy to prevail and even gloat over his undoing. David was possibly overcome with a profound sense of injustice. How could God allow evil to triumph over one who had passionately pursued righteousness? The age-old question resounds: Why do bad things happen to good people?

David was on his face.

The Petition

Perhaps feeling somewhat relieved by his outburst of frustration in the opening verses, David next calmed himself in prayer:

> *Consider* and *answer* me, O Lord my God;
> *Enlighten* my eyes, or I will sleep the sleep of death,
> And my enemy will say, "I have overcome him,"
> And my adversaries will rejoice when I am shaken.
> (vv. 3–4, emphasis added)

David's petition to the Lord was threefold.

Look at me, Lord! David asked the Lord to look at or *consider* anew his situation. He felt the remedy for a sense of abandonment and rejection would be divine attention to his urgent condition. So David prayed for that. When God considers our situations, He cannot help but do so graciously. So one look from the Lord would restore favor and vitality to David's gloomy plight.[4]

Answer me, Lord! Second, David asked for answers. He clearly needed the Lord to act on his behalf, because his very soul was in anguish and he was looking for divine relief from his misery. Apart from God's reassuring presence, David was left to expect the worst imaginable ending: death and humiliation. No doubt he hoped for a word from heaven concerning his ultimate fate.

Enlighten my eyes, Lord! This Hebrew idiom relates to the Lord's blessing. David's eyes had grown dim from the turmoil within, but fresh light for his eyes would be a sign of God's gracious intervention. As commentator Willem A. VanGemeren explains: "A man relieved from troubles and blessed with God's protection, peace, and favor shows his inner spiritual condition in his outward appearance. . . . His eyes sparkle with God's grace."[5]

---

4. See VanGemeren, "Psalms," p. 141.

5. VanGemeren, "Psalms," p. 141.

Perhaps David's ultimate anxiety was betrayed in the parallel lines of verse 4:

> And my enemy will say, "I have overcome him,"
> And my adversaries will rejoice when I am shaken.

If David were overcome by his crisis, his adversaries would have an unbridled opportunity to gloat over the doom of a faithful man. The Lord must absolutely intervene before the godless had time to prepare their victory celebration. For David, his honor and the Lord's glory were visibly at stake.

David was on his knees.

The Praise

David's sudden shift in tone in verses 5–6 shows that his focus was no longer on the gloomy shadows of perilous circumstances. Rather, his gaze was now firmly fixed on the Lord:

> But I have trusted in Your lovingkindness;
> My heart shall rejoice in Your salvation.
> I will sing to the Lord,
> Because He has dealt bountifully with me.

What happened between verses 3–4 and verses 5–6? Nothing indicates that David's circumstances changed for the better. What changed was David's heart. Through prayer, he was able to recall God's unfailing love and care, and he set his heart on that instead of on his troubles. He may have begun his prayer by complaining about what he thought was God's lackluster concern, but he ended it by confessing his confidence in God's faithfulness. As Martin Luther said of David's song, "Hope despairs and yet despair hopes."[6]

David's despair turned to hope as he expressed abounding confidence in the Lord's lovingkindness. He even felt compelled to "sing" of the grand and glorious hope of God's salvation, because the Lord had "dealt bountifully" on his behalf. VanGemeren tells us,

> The verb *gamal* ("deal bountifully with," "reward"; NIV, "has been good") is fraught with meaning. Yahweh bestows his benefits, not in small measure, but in fullness, so as to give his children the experience of complete and free deliverance.[7]

---

6. Martin Luther, as quoted by VanGemeren in "Psalms," p. 139.

7. VanGemeren, "Psalms," p. 142.

Not only did God move on David's behalf, but He moved bountifully so! And David was back on his feet, singing songs of praise to the Lord.

The Application: What Lessons Linger?

Though one of the shortest psalms in the collection, Psalm 13 affords some powerful lessons for believers facing adversity.

First, *during trials, God would rather change us than change our circumstances.* Often, God transforms our lives most powerfully in the crucible of crisis. Because we tend to rely on our own strength and resources for living, it is not until those supplies run thin, or are exhausted, that we realize our need to depend on the Lord. When we let Him do His work, we become more patient, trusting, loving, compassionate. We change, like David did.

And second, *deliverance from any crisis is an act of God's grace.* However God decides to meet our needs, whether urgent or routine, He does so out of a heart of pure grace. He simply cannot act any other way. His grace is always free, undeserved, and beyond what we could ever imagine. No matter our perceived need— financial, physical, emotional, or otherwise—our ultimate need is a dispensing of God's grace.

As you let David's song enter your life more deeply, take these encouraging words from James Montgomery Boice with you:

> If you are suffering from a sense of feeling abandoned by God, which is what this psalm is about, I cannot tell you when the emotional oppression will lift. But it will lift. The curtain of your despair will rise, and behind the veil you will see the blessed Lord Jesus Christ, who has been with you and has loved you all the time.[8]

 *Living Insights*

No matter where we come from, how we were raised, what our occupation, or what our taste in music, one thing is common to us all: adversity. Live long enough, and the winds begin to blow, clouds roll in, and, before you know it, you're facing the storm of your life.

8. Boice, *Psalms (Volume 1, Psalms 1–41)*, p. 112.

For some, it's the frightening uncertainty of cancer. Others face years of loneliness following the death of a mate or a difficult divorce. For still others, it's less tangible—a gradual coldness or hardening of the heart toward the things of the Lord.

Crises that last only a day or two tend to seem endurable. But the ones that linger and increase in intensity often cause despair and anguish—for even the most stalwart of souls.

So, what are we to do in times of crisis? Psalm 13 gives the answer: Pray.

Psalm 13 is really about how to pray in times of crisis. David would have us dispense with all the politeness and conventions of traditional prayer and be honest with the Lord, trusting Him to respond.

Let's do some reflection.

What surprised you about David's prayer in Psalm 13?

_____

_____

_____

_____

_____

Is there any difference in the way David addressed the Lord in verse 1 and how he addressed Him in verse 3? If so, what might be the significance?

_____

_____

_____

_____

_____

List some lessons you can learn about prayer from David's psalm.

_____

_____

_____

_____

_____

How has the Lord answered your prayers in times of crisis? Be specific.

_____

_____

_____

_____

_____

Now, before you go on to the next chapter, take some time to write down the names of a few individuals who are in the middle of a crisis right now. With Psalm 13 in mind, pray for these individuals regularly, asking the Lord to pour out His grace in their lives.

_____

_____

_____

_____

Perhaps even a brief note of encouragement, letting them know you are praying for them and even directing them to the Psalms, may be appropriate. Trust the Spirit's leading. And don't forget to thank the Lord for His amazing grace!

Chapter 4
A SONG OF SOVEREIGNTY
Psalm 46

E ver felt the ground move under your feet? Know what it's like to pitch from side to side in a small boat on strong seas? Ever had to run for cover, dodge bullets, or duck out of the way of advancing troops? Remarkably, some people around the world could answer "Yes!" to all three questions! However, most of us only imagine such scenes.

Still, everyone, sooner or later, faces trials that take on cataclysmic proportions. Left unchecked, fear runs its course and has a way of bringing us to a point of helplessness. If you've ever felt the pinch of life's uncertainty, or if you're stuck between a rock and a hard place, then Psalm 46 is for you.

This psalm is a message of help for the helpless. No matter how bad life may seem, God is in control. He is sovereign. And because He's sovereign, He's a perfect refuge—a place to hide when life comes unglued.

Why is God's sovereignty such a help to us? Let's explore this characteristic of the Lord, and then we'll see in Psalm 46 how His sovereign power puts our fears to rest and instills triumphant confidence.

What Is Sovereignty?

God's sovereignty is His supreme authority in the universe— He reigns over every event and individual with absolute control (see Dan. 4:17, 25, 35; 1 Tim. 6:15). Several of His attributes contribute to His sovereignty: His *omniscience* means that He knows everything—past, present, and future—and that He has unlimited understanding and wisdom. His *omnipotence* gives Him complete power to do whatever He wishes. His *omnipresence* means that no place or person is out of His sight or beyond His reach. And His *eternal nature* makes Him unbounded by any of time's constraints. So, because He is all-knowing, all-powerful, everywhere-present, and everlasting, He is sovereign.

Though God's sovereignty weaves its way through His dealings with His creation, the actual word rarely appears in Scripture. One instance where it is used is in Psalm 103:19:

The Lord has established His throne in the heavens,
And His *sovereignty* rules over all. (emphasis added)

Nothing takes God by surprise! He does everything according to His own will (see Eph. 1:11). This thought is echoed in Psalm 115:3:

But our God is in the heavens;
He does whatever He pleases.

God is perfectly holy, perfectly in control, and therefore perfectly reliable. That's sovereignty. That's God. And that's the foundation on which Psalm 46 was composed.

Psalm 46: The Sovereign God Delivers Us

What might this song have sounded like? One word in the superscription may give us a clue:

For the choir director. A Psalm of the sons of Korah,
set to *Alamoth*. A Song. (emphasis added)

The word *alamoth* carries the thought of "soprano voices of young women," indicating that this psalm could have been composed for women's voices or was possibly accompanied by instruments tuned to maidenlike or high-pitched tones. Perhaps it sounded like the sobbing violins in Samuel Barber's *Adagio for Strings*, reflecting the high-strung fears and feelings of a distressed people. Or maybe it soared with the joy of the "Hallelujah Chorus," celebrating the power and victory of God. We don't really know what direction those soprano tones took.

But we do know that Martin Luther heard strength in it and based his powerful hymn "A Mighty Fortress Is Our God" on this psalm. Certainly, the psalmist sought to lead us to confidence in God's deliverance and ultimate triumph, no matter what life brings our way.

Psalm 46 opens with a confession of trust in our strong God (v. 1), which is echoed by two affirming refrains or confessions that follow the second and third stanzas (vv. 7, 11). Perhaps the choral leader sang the stanzas and the chorus and congregation sang the refrains, making this an antiphonal anthem of praise.

One thing to notice especially is that Psalm 46 begins and ends with the focus firmly on God—a subtle lesson on where to turn for help in times of trouble. With this bird's-eye view in mind, let's take a closer look at each stanza of this reassuring psalm.

We Need Not Fear

The psalmist began with a confession of heartfelt trust in the Lord—the theme—which is followed by a stanza that affirms this confidence in God.[1]

> God is our refuge and strength,
> A very present help in trouble.
> Therefore we will not fear, though the earth should
>   change
> And though the mountains slip into the heart of
>   the sea;
> Though its waters roar and foam,
> Though the mountains quake at its swelling pride.
>
> Selah[2]
>
> (vv. 1–3)

According to these verses, not only is God the perfect source of protection and help in calamity, but He also provides the abiding inner strength necessary to endure life's most daunting odds.[3] And He is willing and eager to assist us when we suffer various ills. James Montgomery Boice says it well:

> God is our help even if the worst imaginable calamities should come upon us. This is what verses 2–3 are about, as the psalmist imagines the return of chaos, in which the "earth gives way and the mountains fall into the heart of the sea," thus reversing the work of God on the third day of creation. Sometimes life is like that. The foundations of our established worlds are shaken, and chaos seems to have come again.[4]

---

1. This section has been adapted from "Growing through Weakness" in the Bible study guide *Growing Pains*, rev. ed., from the Bible-teaching ministry of Charles R. Swindoll (Anaheim, Calif.: Insight for Living, 1999), pp. 47–50.

2. Each of this psalm's three stanzas ends with the Hebrew word *selah*. Though its exact meaning is uncertain, the word seems to act as a musical notation signifying a reflective pause or a change in dynamics or tempo.

3. See James Montgomery Boice, *Psalms: An Expositional Commentary (Volume 2, Psalms 42–106)* (Grand Rapids, Mich.: Baker Book House, 1996), p. 389.

4. Boice, *Psalms (Volume 2, Psalms 42–106)*, p. 389.

In those times, we don't need to be afraid, because God shelters us, strengthens us, and stays close to us. He helps and protects us in times of trouble, and He is 100 percent reliable.

We Will Not Be Moved

The second stanza continues the theme of relying on God's strong presence, but it leaves the forces of nature behind and zooms in on Jerusalem, the city of God, which represents those who are in a covenant relationship with Him. For the people of faith, God's presence brings comfort amid the darkest of circumstances. Notice the striking images in the following verses:

> There is a river whose streams make glad the city
>   of God,
> The holy dwelling places of the Most High.
> God is in the midst of her, she will not be moved;
> God will help her when morning dawns.
> The nations made an uproar, the kingdoms tottered;
> He raised His voice, the earth melted.
> The Lord of hosts is with us;
> The God of Jacob is our stronghold. (vv. 4–7)

Reminiscent of the river in the Garden of Eden (Gen. 2:10), this "river whose streams make glad" symbolizes the restorative flow of God's healing and life-giving grace (see Ezek. 47:1–12; Rev. 22:1–2).[5] Where God is present, there is blessing and joy, and God has promised His presence with us. Because the all-powerful, Most High God is with His people, they shall be secure. Even in life's darkest hour, when everything seems to be in complete disarray, God's presence makes the difference. Let the nations roar and even attack at dawn—God will be right there to protect His people. His voice "will be as decisive in dissolving the world as it was in creating it."[6] Come what may, God and His angels will rally to His people, and He will lift them beyond their enemies' reach.

---

5. See Willem A. VanGemeren, "Psalms," in *The Expositor's Bible Commentary*, gen. ed. Frank E. Gaebelein (Grand Rapids, Mich.: Zondervan Publishing House, 1991), vol. 5, p. 352; and Franz Delitzsch, *Psalms*, vol. 5 of *Commentary on the Old Testament in Ten Volumes* (reprint, Grand Rapids, Mich.: William B. Eerdmans Publishing Co., 1982), p. 94.

6. Derek Kidner, *Psalms 1–72: An Introduction and Commentary on Books I and II of the Psalms*, The Tyndale Old Testament Commentaries Series (Downers Grove, Ill.: InterVarsity Press, 1973), p. 176.

We Don't Need to Strive

The closing verses of Psalm 46 urge us to "Come, behold the works of the Lord" (v. 8a)—to look at and ponder what God has done and will do. As God's people review His faithful acts, they are encouraged by the evidence of His care, protection, and sovereign control.[7] And His enemies come face-to-face with the one true and sovereign God:

> [He] has wrought desolations in the earth.
> He makes wars to cease to the end of the earth;
> He breaks the bow and cuts the spear in two;
> He burns the chariots with fire. (vv. 8b–9)

The "desolations" are those events wrought by God's righteous judgments against people who perpetuate evil, violence, and war on the earth. The Lord will utterly destroy every evil foe, along with their weapons of warfare, and bring lasting peace to the world. No wonder God Himself decided to speak in the next verse:

> "Cease striving and know that I am God;
> I will be exalted among the nations, I will be exalted
> in the earth." (v. 10)

God says, "*Raphah*—Let alone! Do nothing! Be quiet!"[8] The Lord could be saying this to the nations hostile to Him and His people, as commentator Franz Delitzsch paraphrases:

> Cease, cries He . . . to the nations, from making war upon My people, and know that I am God, the invincible One,—invincible both in Myself and in My people,—who will be acknowledged in My exaltation by all the world.[9]

Or the Lord could be addressing His people, urging them to relax in the knowledge that He is sovereign and He is in control—that He will triumph. Charles Spurgeon captures both angles:

7. VanGemeren, "Psalms," p. 353.

8. Francis Brown, S. R. Driver, and Charles A. Briggs, *The New Brown—Driver—Briggs—Gesenius Hebrew and English Lexicon* (Peabody, Mass.: Hendrickson Publishers, 1979), p. 952.

9. Delitzsch, *Psalms*, p. 96. See also Boice, *Psalms (Volume 2, Psalms 42–106)*, p. 392; Kidner, *Psalms 1–72*, p. 176; and A. F. Kirkpatrick, *The Book of Psalms* (1902; reprint, Grand Rapids, Mich.: Baker Book House, 1982), p. 258.

Hold off your hands, ye enemies! Sit down and wait in patience, ye believers! Acknowledge that Jehovah is God, ye who feel the terrors of his wrath! Adore him, and him only, ye who partake in the protections of his grace.[10]

When we rest in who God is and what He is able to do for us, then we can confess with the psalmist,

> The Lord of hosts is with *us*;
> The God of Jacob is *our* stronghold.
> (v. 11, emphasis added)

Closing Thoughts

Tired of striving? Concerned about the future? Great! You're right where God wants you to be—ready to accept His help and strength. Sometimes He allows us to get to the very end of our rope to help us discover that He's what we've needed all along.

Perhaps that's why Martin Luther included the following stanza in his great hymn "A Mighty Fortress Is Our God":

> Did we in our own strength confide,
> Our striving would be losing,
> Were not the right man on our side,
> The man of God's own choosing.
> Dost ask who that may be?
> Christ Jesus, it is He—
> Lord Sabaoth His name,
> From age to age the same,
> And He must win the battle.[11]

Facing the battle of your life? Cease striving. You have a Savior, and He's on your side. Let Him win this one for you!

10. C. H. Spurgeon, *The Treasury of David* (McLean, Va.: MacDonald Publishing Co., n.d.), vol. 1, p. 343.

11. Martin Luther, "A Mighty Fortress Is Our God," in *The Hymnal for Worship and Celebration* (Waco, Tex.: Word Music, 1986), no. 26.

 *Living Insights*

From Psalm 46, we can prescribe a good remedy for despair during troubled times: reflect on God's past faithfulness to us. If we think long and hard enough, we begin to realize just how many times He's come through for us.

Take some time to reflect on the past year, month, or even week. In the space provided, list some specific occasions when the Lord came through for you in a tight place.

_____

_____

_____

_____

_____

_____

_____

_____

_____

_____

Does fear hinder you from experiencing God's blessing? How?

_____

_____

_____

_____

_____

_____

What truths has Psalm 46 taught you about God's character that could help you face life's inevitable difficulties?

_____

_____

_____

_____

_____

_____

_____

_____

In the event that a close friend or loved one should come to you, desperate and discouraged because of a crisis he or she is facing, what sort of advice would you give?

_____

_____

_____

_____

_____

_____

_____

_____

_____

Chapter 5

TWO SONGS FOR MOMS AND DADS

Psalms 127–128

Let's face it, families today are in trouble. Our society used to honor traditional values like faithfulness, honesty, integrity, moral purity, and kindness, but now it seems indifferent, and sometimes even hostile, to the mainstays that once promised stability.

To make matters worse, the average family spends little time actually *being* a family. The race to keep pace with technology, the pressure to be involved in every extracurricular activity imaginable, and the drive to possess more and more stuff all splinter off valuable hours for investing in what matters most at home.

Like ships with faulty rudders, families end up lost at sea. Something is missing. *Someone* is missing. And that someone is God.

No matter what the endeavor, without Him as our guide, we'll veer off course sooner or later. Wave after wave of frustration will slam against our tattered hulls until our families splinter and our hearts break. Ultimately, we'll drift rudderless, starved for intimacy and parched for happiness.

Do you need to put the Lord at the helm of your family? You'll find the encouragement you need to do just that in Psalms 127 and 128—two psalms that show the blessings that come with keeping the Lord at the center of your life. And remember, it's never too late to start doing what's right—with God, all things are possible (Matt. 19:26; Luke 1:37). Let's pull into the quiet harbor of God's Word, then, and learn the importance of letting God be in control.

Without the Lord, Emptiness (Psalm 127)

Let's look first at Psalm 127. James Montgomery Boice crystallizes its theme for us: "A Latin motto says, *Nisi Dominus Frustra*. It comes from the first words of this psalm and means 'Without the Lord, Frustration.' . . . It could be attached to the lives of many who are trying to live their lives without the Almighty."[1] Solomon,

---

1. James Montgomery Boice, *Psalms: An Expositional Commentary* (Volume 3, Psalms 107–150) (Grand Rapids, Mich.: Baker Books, 1998), p. 1118.

the author of this psalm, would have known this better than most. When his heart was no longer wholly the Lord's, everything he tried to do in life was marked by emptiness and frustration (see Ecclesiastes).

Our Frantic Efforts

Solomon opened Psalm 127 with a warning:

> Unless the Lord builds the house,
> They labor in vain who build it;
> Unless the Lord guards the city,
> The watchman keeps awake in vain. (v. 1)

If God is not guiding each endeavor, everything we do has little or no value—our efforts don't lead anywhere. The Lord must remain the essential factor in any undertaking—from building a home or family to protecting a community. Without Him, happiness and security are a mirage, because He "is the central reality of all existence."[2]

So Solomon said that there is no separating the prosperous home or safely guarded city from God's gracious superintending. Prosperity and protection come from His hand. To deny Him access to either home or city is to forfeit blessing and invite disaster.

The same is true for our families today. In the busyness of starting a family, it's easy to lose sight of what really matters: our relationship with the Lord. Often in the early years of marriage, during the inception of the home, a couple sacrifices time with the Lord and with each other on the altar of their careers. They get trapped into believing that by working longer hours, advancing further upwards, and accumulating nicer things, they'll increase their chances for happiness. But once God loses His place in our daily routine—especially in our relationships with our spouses—survival eventually becomes the dominant mode. Thankfully, Solomon told us the truth:

> It is vain for you to rise up early,
> To retire late,
> To eat the bread of painful labors;
> For He gives to His beloved even in his sleep. (v. 2)

---

2. Eugene H. Peterson, *A Long Obedience in the Same Direction* (Downers Grove, Ill.: Inter-Varsity Press, 1980), p. 104.

Driving ambition is not the way to genuine fulfillment! Pursuing God's best is what guarantees real happiness—at work and at home. Trusting Him to bless and protect our work and family is the straighter course to chart. In fact, even in what most people consider to be the most unproductive hours—nighttime—God dispenses grace to His children (v. 2b).

God's Gracious Gifts

In contrast to our attempts at self-sufficiency is the quiet miracle of life bestowed by the Giver of life:[3]

> Behold, children are a gift of the Lord,
> The fruit of the womb is a reward. (v. 3)

Solomon used two words in these parallel lines to describe the blessing of children: They are a *gift* and a *reward*. The word *gift* in Hebrew means "possession, property, inheritance." In the margin of the NASB, an alternate word is given: *heritage*. And John H. Stek, in *The NIV Study Bible*, further illuminates the idea for us:

> In the OT economy, an Israelite's "inheritance" from
> the Lord was first of all property in the promised land,
> . . . which provided a sure place in the life and "rest"
> . . . of the Lord's kingdom. But without children
> the inheritance in the land would be lost, . . . so
> that offspring were a heritage in a double sense.[4]

The second word, *reward*, in this context, echoes the meaning wrapped up in *gift*—it is another pointer to God's initiative and generosity.

So God has given to our families the children He created—they come from His hand of grace, not just our human efforts. We should not regard our children, then, as mistakes, accidents, interruptions, or even tax deductions! They are a reflection of the Lord's kindness and blessing. When we raise our children with this awareness, we

---

3. Derek Kidner adds this insightful observation: "God's gifts are as unpretentious as they are miraculous. The two halves of the psalm are neatly illustrated by the first and last paragraphs of Genesis 11, where man builds for glory and security, to achieve only a fiasco, whereas God quietly gives to the obscure Terah a son [Abraham] whose blessings have proliferated ever since." *Psalms 73–150: A Commentary on Books III–V of the Psalms*, The Tyndale Old Testament Commentaries Series (Downers Grove, Ill.: InterVarsity Press, 1975), p. 441.

4. John H. Stek, note on Psalm 127:3, in *The NIV Study Bible*, gen. ed. Kenneth L. Barker (Grand Rapids, Mich.: Zondervan Bible Publishers, 1985), p. 925.

honor the Lord who gave them to us. And when they grow up to become godly adults, we have passed along the heritage of blessing to the next generation.

By bestowing children, the Lord builds our house and guards our city too:

> Like arrows in the hand of a warrior,
> So are the children of one's youth.
> How blessed is the man whose quiver is full of them;
> They will not be ashamed
> When they speak with their enemies in the gate.
> (vv. 4–5)

Most of us today don't need to carry around a quiver of sharpened arrows or contend for justice at our city gate (most of us probably don't even have a city gate!). So it will help us to understand this blessing from a historical perspective. Theologians J. W. Rogerson and J. W. McKay explain:

> In an agricultural society, a large number of children will help to defend and work the family lands. The psalmist, however, sees the greatest benefit as accruing in the field of justice, where cases were heard in the gate of the city. . . . Whereas in corrupt times justice might be denied to the defenceless (e.g. the widow and orphan) it would hardly be denied to a man backed by a number of hefty sons![5]

In our society, we can draw from these images the idea of how important godly children are to parents facing the challenges of growing older. If we maintain loving, healthy relationships with our children, we will be able to count on them to be our advocates— especially when it comes to medical care—and to guard us against the loneliness and abandonment that often accompany old age.[6]

Eugene Peterson provides an additional insight: "People are at the center of Christian work. . . . The character of our work is shaped not by accomplishments or possessions but in the birth of

---

5. J. W. Rogerson and J. W. McKay, *Psalms 101–150*, The Cambridge Bible Commentary Series (London, England: Cambridge University Press, 1977), p. 127.

6. See Willem A. VanGemeren, "Psalms," in *The Expositor's Bible Commentary*, gen. ed. Frank E. Gaebelein (Grand Rapids, Mich.: Zondervan Publishing House, 1991), vol. 5, p. 795.

relationships: 'Sons are a heritage from the Lord.' We invest our energy in people."[7]

With the Lord, Happiness (Psalm 128)

While Psalm 127 starts with a negative example, Psalm 128 opens with God's blessings on wise living. And though Psalm 127 convinces us that all blessings are attributed to God, Psalm 128 shows us the necessary responsibilities we must embrace in order to partake of those blessings—fearing the Lord and walking in His ways.[8] The benefits of walking in obedience to God are far-reaching, as Derek Kidner explains:

> The quiet blessings of an ordered life are traced from the centre outwards in this psalm, as the eye travels from the godly man to his family and finally to Israel. Here is simple piety with its proper fruit of stability and peace.[9]

Let's see how we can steer our families toward blessing from the wisdom in this psalm.

Blessings for Those Who Fear the Lord

There is only one route leading to genuine blessing in life: the route of faith. And that faith is expressed through fearing God (reverence) and walking in His ways (obedience):

> How blessed is everyone who fears the Lord,
> Who walks in His ways. (v. 1)

Eugene Peterson helps us understand more deeply what it means to fear the Lord:

> The Bible isn't interested in whether we believe in God or not. It assumes that everyone more or less does. What it is interested in is the response we have toward him: will we let God be as he is, majestic and holy, vast and wondrous, or will we always be trying to whittle him down to the size of our small

7. Peterson, *A Long Obedience in the Same Direction*, p. 106.
8. See Boice, *Psalms (Volume 3, Psalms 107–150)*, p. 1124.
9. Kidner, *Psalms 73–150*, p. 443.

37

minds, insist on confining him within the boundaries we are comfortable with, refuse to think of him other than in images that are convenient to our lifestyle? But then we are not dealing with the God of creation and the Christ of the cross, but with a dime-store reproduction of something made in our image, usually for commercial reasons. To guard against all such blasphemous chumminess with the Almighty, the Bible talks of the fear of the Lord—not to scare us but to bring us to awesome attention before the overwhelming grandeur of God, to shut up our whining and chattering and stop our running and fidgeting so that we can really see him as he is and listen to him as he speaks his merciful, life-changing words of forgiveness.[10]

How do we walk in God's ways? Again, Peterson illuminates the psalmist's wisdom for us:

We not only let God be God as he really is, but we start doing the things for which he made us. We take a certain route; we follow certain directions; we do specified things. There are ethical standards to follow, there are moral values to foster, there are spiritual disciplines to practice, there is social justice to pursue, there are personal relationships to develop.[11]

Life is more difficult when we abandon God's ways for our own. But when we follow Him faithfully, He gives us more joy in life:

When you shall eat of the fruit of your hands,
You will be happy and it will be well with you. (v. 2)

The Lord's blessing first comes in a profound satisfaction in our work. That work translates into God's provision for us and our families. Our proper response is gratitude coupled with a trust that knows the Lord will meet all our needs.

We need to train up our children in this kind of faith, because God rewards people who keep Him at the center of their lives and

10. Peterson, *A Long Obedience in the Same Direction*, p. 116.

11. Peterson, *A Long Obedience in the Same Direction*, p. 116.

gladly submit to Him. Learning these lessons will help our families flourish; indeed, respect and obedience are the first things children must master if they are to live successfully in the home and beyond it.

The psalm goes on to explain the ways in which God blesses the families of those who reverently obey Him:

> Your wife shall be like a fruitful vine
> Within your house,
> Your children like olive plants
> Around your table.
> Behold, for thus shall the man be blessed
> Who fears the Lord. (vv. 3–4)

The entire family reaps the rewards of faithfulness! The mother finds fulfillment in her role as a wife and as a source of love and nurture (the vine), and the children, full of promise and potential (olive shoots), learn to walk faithfully with God. Both the vine and the olive are rich biblical symbols for the abundant life. Only those who choose to stay God's course experience that abundance.[12]

Benediction for the Blessed

The final verses of Psalm 128 serve as a benediction. Originally pronounced upon pilgrim families leaving Jerusalem, this blessing applies to all who seek to serve the Lord and walk with Him:

> The Lord bless you from Zion,
> And may you see the prosperity of Jerusalem all the
> days of your life.
> Indeed, may you see your children's children.
> Peace be upon Israel! (vv. 5–6)

Willem A. VanGemeren unfolds the significance of this blessing:

> The blessing of God also extends to the prosper-
> ity of Jerusalem. The godly person in the OT was
> not only concerned about his personal well-being or
> the well-being of his family; but, while away from
> the temple, he was concerned also about the worship

---

12. See Boice, *Psalms (Volume 3, Psalms 107–150)*, p. 1128. Boice adds some significant information about the olive tree image: "Patiently cultivated, they become quite valuable and continue to produce a profitable crop for centuries, longer perhaps than any other fruit-producing tree or plant."

of God, the defense of the city of Jerusalem, and the welfare of the Davidic dynasty. He knew that if a godly king were ruling over Jerusalem, and if godly priests were serving in the temple, God's blessing would extend to his people.[13]

How does this apply to us today? This benediction shows us that our families are part of a greater drama. "What is meant is that the family must not be an end in itself. We should not live only for our family. All families of believers should gladly share in God's plan for the redemption of the world."[14] We need to be teaching our families to look outward and work for the welfare of God's kingdom in this world.

After praying that we would have a long life to enjoy God's many blessings ("may you see your children's children"), the psalmist closed his song with a prayer for peace for the faith community. The ultimate blessing for all, of course, comes in the reality of eternal peace, which will be ushered in when finally God "will wipe away every tear from [our] eyes" (Rev. 21:4).

Then we shall be blessed indeed!

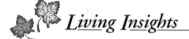 *Living Insights*

Getting our families back on course takes some reflection. The psalmists wanted us to examine the place God holds in our individual lives and in the everyday lives of our families. Take some time right now to reflect on both areas, getting as accurate a picture as you can.

Priority #1: Your God

Is the Lord your first priority? Do you have a healthy fear of Him, regarding Him with reverence and awe? Are you committed to walking in His ways? Do you have established patterns of prayer and study in His Word? Does He take first place in your business? Your ministry? Your political, financial, and social decisions? Do

13. VanGemeren, "Psalms," p. 797.

14. George A. F. Knight, *Psalms*, vol. 2, The Daily Study Bible Series (Philadelphia, Pa.: Westminster Press, 1983), p. 283.

you worship Him regularly? Are you committed to being in church on a regular basis?

In the space provided, list some areas where you sense you've veered from God's charted course.

_____

_____

_____

_____

_____

Priority #2: Your Family

How is your relationship with your spouse? Does your husband or wife receive the time and care he or she needs and deserves? Are you praying together? Spending undistracted time together?

What about your children? Where do they rank on your list of what matters most? Are you investing time in their lives so they'll reverence the Lord and walk in His ways when they are grown? Are you as a family committed to being regularly involved in a church?

Again, write down some areas where you feel you've drifted from God's best.

_____

_____

_____

_____

Now ask yourself one final question: Am I trying to bless myself, or am I really allowing the Lord to bless my family and me?

_____

_____

_____

It's all about getting back on course—God's course—for you and your family. And it's never too late to start doing what's right!

Chapter 6

A SONG OF REASSURANCE
Psalm 139

How fitting that our study in God's Songbook should end on the high note of Psalm 139! This psalm celebrates God as the omniscient and omnipresent Lord, the Creator-God, and the Holy One. But the psalmist, David, didn't praise God for merely abstract qualities—he saw how incredibly near and personal the almighty God is. As J. A. Motyer explains,

> To the psalmist omniscience is God's complete knowledge of me; omnipresence, God with me in every place; creatorship, God's sovereign ownership of every part of me; and holiness, God's will that I be like him.[1]

And Derek Kidner promises that "any small thoughts that we may have of God are magnificently transcended by this psalm; yet for all its height and depth it remains intensely personal from first to last."[2]

The God of the Holy Scriptures is an "intensely personal" God— a much-needed truth in our day. So many forces conspire to make us feel unseen, unimportant, insignificant, uncared for. Voice mail programs wend us through a labyrinth of recorded choices that keep us from speaking with another human being. Software programs replace us at work, supposedly doing our jobs faster and cheaper. Some churches get so big that we can attend for years and still remain anonymous. And busyness erodes our relationships, stealing the time we need to really know and be known by those we love.

Our world can be terribly impersonal, can't it? It can make us wonder if we really matter, if there's any purpose to our being here.

Insight for Living gratefully acknowledges Ray C. Stedman's book *Psalms of Faith: A Life-Related Study from Selected Psalms*, rev. ed. (Ventura, Calif.: Gospel Light Publications, Regal Books, 1988), pp. 306–15, in the development of this sermon's theme and the exposition of verses 1–15.

1. J. A. Motyer, "The Psalms," in *New Bible Commentary: 21st Century Edition*, 4th ed., edited by D. A. Carson, R. T. France, J. A. Motyer, and G. J. Wenham (Downers Grove, Ill.: InterVarsity Press, 1994), p. 578.

2. Derek Kidner, *Psalms 73–150: A Commentary on Books III–V of the Psalms*, The Tyndale Old Testament Commentaries Series (Downers Grove, Ill.: InterVarsity Press, 1975), p. 463.

Psalm 139 tells us that we *do* matter—to the most important One in this world or any: God. He doesn't look without really seeing us; He watches over us intently. He doesn't listen without really hearing us; He probes the deepest recesses of our hearts. If we try to think of some possible place or situation that's beyond His reach, His loving face is already there, waiting for us.

As we prepare to learn the melody of this last song in our study, quiet your mind and heart. Silence those messages from the world that tell you that you don't matter. And listen to God's truth instead, resting and delighting in His care, as David did.

An Overview of Psalm 139

Let's get oriented to this beautiful psalm by understanding why David may have written it, how he structured and developed his thoughts, and what approach he took to express his prayer to the Lord.

The Occasion

Though no one knows for certain when or why this psalm was written, some conservative scholars believe that verses 19–24 give us a clue. J. A. Motyer asserts that "the tension between the psalmist and the wicked in 19–24 must be the setting from which the psalm sprang," adding that

> some situation of moral conflict, evil in its most culpable (19) and outrageous (20–21) forms, made David not only take sides (19–24) but also re-explore his shelter and security in God (1–18). . . . [The psalm's] theology is undatable [but] perfectly at home in the mouth and experience of David.[3]

Commentator Leslie C. Allen concurs, supplying a few extra details:

> The speaker of the psalm has come to the sanctuary to present his prayer, hoping for a divine oracle to vindicate him. He protests his innocence of certain charges evidently brought against him, before Yahweh who has insight into the whole of his life. . . . The psalmist is in some situation of attack. The

3. Motyer, "The Psalms," p. 578.

psalm is comparable with Jeremiah's appeal for vindication: "You know me, Yahweh; you see me and probe my attitude toward you. Pull them out like sheep for the slaughter" (Jer 12:3; cf. 15:15). The psalmist is . . . pleading for justice to be done.[4]

David needed the reassurance that God saw the truth of his devotion to Him. And he found it not only by trusting the Lord to answer his cry but by recalling how well God knows His people . . . and this faithful servant in particular.

The Structure

David put his thoughts into four stanzas that have six verses each, with the ideas in each stanza flowing into the next. J. A. Motyer and Derek Kidner outline Psalm 139 this way:[5]

A. *God is all-seeing and all-knowing* (vv. 1–6). When we feel insignificant and struggle with our identity, we can find reassurance in how closely God pays attention to us and how well He knows us.

B. *God is all-present* (vv. 7–12). When we're lonely and not sure how close God is to us, we'll find in these verses that He is always with us, present and caring.

C. *God is all-creative* (vv. 13–18). When our self-image suffers from unkind comparisons, we can take comfort in how carefully God has made each of us.

D. *God is all-holy* (vv. 19–24). When we worry about evil and its assaults on God's people, we can rest in God's righteousness, guidance, and protection.

David saw that God knew his heart and mind even better than he did (vv. 1–6), and even if he wished to escape the Lord's scrutiny, there was no place he could go where God wouldn't already be present (vv. 7–12). The darkness couldn't hide him either, because God had His hand on David even in the unseen world of the womb (vv. 13–18). God's thoughts were so far above David that he was simply amazed—and he was outraged at anyone who would speak against this marvelous, holy God or His faithful people (vv. 19–24).

---

4. Leslie C. Allen, *Word Biblical Commentary: Psalms 101–150* (Waco, Tex.: Word Books, Publisher, 1983), vol. 21, pp. 260–61.

5. See Motyer, "The Psalms," pp. 578–79; and Kidner, *Psalms 73–150*, pp. 464–67.

With one thought springing off of another, David explored the wonderful and reassuring truths about God's nature. But he wasn't writing a dissertation or an analytical essay—his approach was much more heartfelt than that.

The Approach

David's poem was a prayer—not a formal, memorized prayer but an open, intimate talk with God. David approached the Lord with a unique combination of familiarity and reverence, always preserving the Lord's dignity and never crossing over into presumptuous chumminess.

We need to learn from David's approach. Too often, we treat the Lord as if He's our "buddy" or "our friend the giant." But He is the sovereign Lord, and we need to come before Him with reverence and respect.

Now that we have a grasp of the big picture, let's make a more detailed examination of Psalm 139.

An Examination of Psalm 139

David's psalm opens with a description of the Lord's omniscience —He sees and knows everything about us.

God Knows Us Intimately

> O Lord, You have searched me and known me.
> You know when I sit down and when I rise up;
> You understand my thought from afar.
> You scrutinize my path and my lying down,
> And are intimately acquainted with all my ways.
> Even before there is a word on my tongue,
> Behold, O Lord, You know it all.
> You have enclosed me behind and before,
> And laid Your hand upon me. (Ps. 139:1–5)

"Lord," David was basically saying, "You have diligently probed my character and have discerned my actions and the motives behind them."[6] Whether David was sitting or standing, going out or coming

---

6. The Hebrew word for *searched, chaqar,* "connotes a diligent, difficult probing . . . often [of] a person's character or feelings." The word *known, yada,* has "to discern" and "to recognize" as its synonyms. R. Laird Harris, Gleason L. Archer Jr., and Bruce K. Waltke, eds., *Theological Wordbook of the Old Testament* (Chicago, Ill.: Moody Press, 1980), vol. 1, pp. 318, 366.

in, God had a perfect understanding of his everyday activities as well as his most private thoughts. In scrutinizing David's path, the Lord was actually winnowing or measuring his lifestyle.[7] Every action, every motive, was carefully and painstakingly overseen by God. Before David could form a word, the Lord knew his full meaning. As commentator George A. F. Knight paraphrases David's words,

> You know every detail about the flow of my sentences, their superficial sound, their real meaning, their connection with my attitude to life, my faith, or even my lack of it.[8]

The Lord was "behind and before" David, guiding him with His hand of protection and love[9] (v. 5). For David, God's perfect knowledge and all-seeing eye were a continual source of comfort. But if we're honest, we have to admit that it scares us a little sometimes. George A. F. Knight, though, reassures us of the love behind God's watchful eye:

> On some children's bedroom walls in the Victorian era there hung a framed picture of a huge eye, enough to scare the wits out of a sensitive child; for underneath the frame were the words: "Thou Lord seest me." . . . But as we proceed to read this powerful psalm, we find that the almighty Eye does not create fear in mankind, far less in little children. It creates an outspilling of love beyond all that the human mind can conceive.[10]

David was in awe of God's infinite and incomprehensible watch over him:

> Such knowledge is too wonderful for me;
> It is too high, I cannot attain to it. (v. 6)

It's as if he was saying, "Too much, Lord! You are beyond the limits of my small mind!" Then he discovered even more.

---

7. See Harris, Archer, and Waltke, *Theological Wordbook of the Old Testament*, vol. 1, p. 251.

8. George A. F. Knight, *Psalms*, vol. 2, The Daily Study Bible Series (Philadelphia, Pa.: Westminster Press, 1983), p. 320.

9. See Motyer, "The Psalms," p. 578.

10. Knight, *Psalms*, p. 320.

God Surrounds Us Constantly

> Where can I go from Your Spirit?
> Or where can I flee from Your presence?
> If I ascend to heaven, You are there;
> If I make my bed in Sheol, behold, You are there.
> If I take the wings of the dawn,
> If I dwell in the remotest part of the sea,
> Even there Your hand will lead me,
> And Your right hand will lay hold of me.
> (vv. 7–10)

"Is there anywhere God is not watching me?" David wondered. And the answer he found was a comforting, "No, He is present with me everywhere." This is God's *omnipresence*, and David found in it a great source of comfort and grace. With a series of rhetorical questions, he exhausted the possible places in heaven and earth where God might not be, but he found that God's presence reaches to every imaginable realm: from the highest places in the heavens to the deepest caverns in the earth ("Sheol"), from the unknown boundaries of the sun ("wings of the dawn") to the remotest point in the ocean. God is not only present, but also active, guiding, and protecting with His own hand (v. 10).

Even the dark could not hide David from the Lord:

> If I say, "Surely the darkness will overwhelm me,
> And the light around me will be night,"
> Even the darkness is not dark to You,
> And the night is as bright as the day.
> Darkness and light are alike to You. (vv. 11–12)

God's presence transcends the darkness. In fact, from God's perspective, there is no darkness—only perfect light (see 1 John 1:5). Not even the hidden world of the womb is beyond God's superintendence, as David next explored.

God Creates Us Perfectly

> For You formed my inward parts;
> You wove me in my mother's womb.
> I will give thanks to You, for I am fearfully and
>   wonderfully made;
> Wonderful are Your works,
> And my soul knows it very well.

My frame was not hidden from You,
When I was made in secret,
And skillfully wrought in the depths of the earth;
Your eyes have seen my unformed substance;
And in Your book were all written
The days that were ordained for me,
When as yet there was not one of them.
(Ps. 139:13–16)

Inspired by the Holy Spirit, David provided a glimpse into the inner workings of a developing fetus.[11] Verse 13 emphasizes that God—not Mother Nature, not chance, not fate—forms us in the womb. The phrase "inward parts" is literally *kidneys,* an image the Hebrews used to represent the whole body and its vital organs, as well as the conscience, emotions, will, and personality.[12] David also said that the Lord "wove" him together, intricately knitting or embroidering a unique design.

Each baby's tiny skeleton ("frame," v. 15) and nerves, blood vessels, muscles, and chemicals ("unformed substance," v. 16a) are "skillfully wrought" by the Lord in the womb ("depths of the earth," v. 16b). Not only that, but as J. A. Motyer explains, David revealed that "every embryo is a person, a creative possession of God with days planned ahead, a life ordained in heaven to be lived on earth."[13] Every detail of our lives has already been written in the Lord's book of life!

The wonder of these magnificent thoughts led David to praise the Lord twice: first in verse 14—"Wonderful are Your works!"—and then in verses 17–18:

How precious also are Your thoughts to me,
    O God!
How vast is the sum of them!
If I should count them, they would outnumber
    the sand.
When I awake, I am still with You.

11. Some stunning examples of life in the womb captured by fiber-optic photography can be found in Lennart Nilsson's book *A Child Is Born,* rev. ed. (New York, N.Y.: Delacorte Press, 1986).

12. See Allen, *Word Biblical Commentary: Psalms 101–150,* p. 251; Motyer, "The Psalms," p. 578; John Stott, *Favorite Psalms* (Chicago, Ill.: Moody Press, 1988), p. 120; and Harris, Archer, and Waltke, *Theological Wordbook of the Old Testament,* vol. 1, pp. 440–41.

13. Motyer, "The Psalms," pp. 578–79.

For David, these truths so far exceeded his grasp that they seemed dreamlike. But they were not a dream—for when he "awakes" in the morning, and when he would awake into the eternal dawn, God would still be there in His perfect power and love.

That anyone would not value the Lord's precious thoughts and person outraged David, and from prayer he turned to imprecation.

God Leads Us Rightly

> O that You would slay the wicked, O God;
> Depart from me, therefore, men of bloodshed.
> For they speak against You wickedly,
> And Your enemies take Your name in vain.
> Do I not hate those who hate You, O Lord?
> And do I not loathe those who rise up against
>   You?
> I hate them with the utmost hatred;
> They have become my enemies. (vv. 19–22)

The evil surrounding David was totally incompatible with the God he had so beautifully extolled. So he used imprecatory language —language that asks the Lord to judge and even curse enemies— to invoke God's justice for the sake of His righteous reputation (compare Ps. 137). It's as if David was saying, "Get rid of those people who incarnate sin!"[14]

Sin is a grievous affront to God's righteous character, and David confronted its awful reality in these verses. Notice, though, that David may have hated those who hated the Lord, but he left justice in God's hands. He didn't start a one-man crusade against evil people; he waited for God to act according to His will.

Furthermore, David remembered that, though he loved the Lord, he wasn't perfect either—he wasn't immune to the sin he confessed to despise. But he was determined to allow the Lord full access to his heart in order to rid himself of sin:

> Search me, O God, and know my heart;
> Try me and know my anxious thoughts;
> And see if there be any hurtful way in me,
> And lead me in the everlasting way. (vv. 23–24)

Essentially, David was asking the Lord to further search and know

---

14. Knight, *Psalms*, p. 326.

him, returning full circle to his theme in verse 1. This time, however, he didn't want personal justification but personal redemption —an everlasting way to freedom from evil. And he wanted the Lord to personally lead him along the everlasting way to life in Himself, the God who created him and is ever near.

Lessons That Linger from Psalm 139

Though the wonderful music of Psalm 139 has ended, its inspiring melody lingers on. So many truths about God's care and closeness wash over our souls, but two overarching lessons will challenge us to reflect deeply on our own lives.

First, *because we are creatures and He is our Creator, we must allow Him to search us and reveal anything in our lives that dishonors Him.* This would include anything from leaving Him out of our lives to not treating others as God's precious creations. Whatever it may be, we need to let God uncover it and lead us into the light of His love and grace.

Second, *the only logical response to God's greatness is to invite Him to lead and have complete control, no matter what that may mean.* This could mean a radical reordering of priorities or finally trusting in Him for your personal salvation. Through the death of His Son, Jesus Christ, God has made a way for you to have eternal freedom from the penalty of sin (see Rom. 6:22–23; Gal. 3:13; Eph. 1:7). Sin is a heart problem that only God can rectify, and the only remedy is faith in Jesus Christ for eternal redemption (see John 1:12; Rom. 10:9–10).

As we wrap up our time in God's Songbook, let's turn to the Lord in prayer, allowing what we've discovered about God's greatness to penetrate our minds and hearts.

> *Our Father, we thank You for telling us how much You thought of us before we were even born. In a world that seems bent on diminishing the significance of life, help us remember and hold on to Your precious thoughts toward us. Guide us daily into gratitude for You and everything You have done for us in Your Son, Jesus Christ.*
>
> *Free us, Father, from any lingering doubts, so we don't spend our lives wondering if we really matter. If You cared enough about us to not only create us but provide for our eternal redemption through the death of Your Son, then we are significant indeed.*

Thank You for the reassurance of this psalm—that
life truly is worth living because of You!
In the dear, precious name of Christ, Amen.

 ## *Living Insights*

So, how does it feel to be the object of all God's affection today? That's right! Despite the fact that He created the universe, holds all things together by His power, and is busy governing the planet, you are His primary concern.

Feeling overwhelmed today? Trying to balance time with your children, your checkbook, and the family meals? Feeling like you're not making a lasting difference in anyone's life? Caught in the trap of comparing yourself and your body to the glamorous models plastered on endless TV commercials and magazine ads? Wondering if any of it matters anyway?

As real as they are, those feelings are rooted in a misunderstanding of God and His perfect plan and purpose for you. That is where Psalm 139 can help. It gives reassurance, tells you that you *do* matter. God designed you Himself for a special purpose. More than that, He knows you intimately and cares about you deeply. He understands your fears, your insecurities, your dreams, and your hopes.

The question is, do you believe Him? He has chosen to reveal Himself to you in His Word and in His Son Jesus Christ. Don't let today end without getting on your knees and thanking Him for who you are, how He made you, and what He's doing in your life. In fact, why not take some time right now to compose your own psalm of praise to the Lord? We have provided space for you to write a prayer that expresses your heart to the Lord—first for who He is, and then for all He has given to you in Christ!

My Psalm of Praise to the Lord

_____

_____

_____

_____

_____

_____

_____

_____

_____

_____

_____

_____

_____

_____

_____

_____

_____

_____

_____

_____

_____

_____

_____

Amen.

BOOKS FOR
PROBING FURTHER

Hopefully, this study has been a source of encouragement to you.
More than that, we pray that it has sparked your interest to
explore more deeply God's magnificent treasure trove of songs: the
book of Psalms.

In order to do that, we suggest you investigate some additional
resources, both scholarly and devotional. You can gain a vast array
of insights from both past and current research on the Psalms. To
help you get started, we have listed a few of these sources below. May
the Lord bless you as you seek to know Him and His Word better!

Commentaries on the Psalms

Boice, James Montgomery. *Psalms: An Expositional Commentary (Volume 1, Psalms 1–41)*. Grand Rapids, Mich.: Baker Books, 1994.

———. *Psalms: An Expositional Commentary (Volume 2, Psalms 42–106)*. Grand Rapids, Mich.: Baker Books, 1996.

———. *Psalms: An Expositional Commentary (Volume 3, Psalms 107–150)*. Grand Rapids, Mich.: Baker Books, 1998.

Brueggemann, Walter. *The Message of the Psalms: A Theological Commentary*. Minneapolis, Minn.: Augsburg Publishing House, 1984.

Craigie, Peter C. *Word Biblical Commentary: Psalms 1–50*. Vol. 19. Waco, Tex.: Word Books, Publisher, 1983.

Kidner, Derek. *Psalms 1–72: An Introduction and Commentary on Books I and II of the Psalms*. The Tyndale Old Testament Commentaries Series. Downers Grove, Ill.: InterVarsity Press, 1973.

———. *Psalms 73–150: A Commentary on Books III–V of the Psalms*. The Tyndale Old Testament Commentaries Series. Downers Grove, Ill.: InterVarsity Press, 1975.

Petersen, David L., and Kent Harold Richards. *Interpreting Hebrew Poetry*. Minneapolis, Minn.: Fortress Press, 1992.

Devotionals on the Psalms

Allen, Ronald Barclay. *Praise! A Matter of Life and Breath*. Nashville, Tenn.: Thomas Nelson Publishers, 1980.

Cole, C. Donald. *Thirsting for God: A Devotional Study of the Psalms, in Light of Their Historical Background*. Westchester, Ill.: Good News Publishers, Crossway Books, 1986.

Peterson, Eugene H. *A Long Obedience in the Same Direction: Discipleship in an Instant Society*. Downers Grove, Ill.: InterVarsity Press, 1980.

Swindoll, Charles R. *Living Beyond the Daily Grind: Reflections on the Songs and Sayings in Scripture*. Books I and II. Dallas, Tex.: Word Publishing, 1988.

Wyrtzen, Don. *A Musician Looks at the Psalms*. Grand Rapids, Mich.: Zondervan Publishing House, 1991.

Some of these books may be out of print and available only through a library. For those currently available, please contact your local Christian bookstore. Books by Charles R. Swindoll, as well as some books by other authors, may be obtained through Insight for Living.

Insight for Living also offers study guides on many books of the Bible, as well as on a variety of issues and biblical personalities. For more information, see the ordering instructions that follow and contact the office that serves you.

NOTES

_____

_____

_____

_____

_____

_____

_____

_____

_____

_____

_____

_____

_____

_____

NOTES

NOTES

NOTES

ORDERING INFORMATION

SONGS FOR ALL SEASONS

If you would like to order additional study guides, purchase the audiocassette series that accompanies this guide, or request our product catalogs, please contact the office that serves you.

United States and International locations:

Insight for Living
Post Office Box 69000
Anaheim, CA 92817-0900

1-800-772-8888, 24 hours a day, seven days a week
(714) 575-5000, 8:00 A.M. to 4:30 P.M., Pacific time, Monday to Friday

Canada:

Insight for Living Ministries
Post Office Box 2510
Vancouver, BC, Canada V6B 3W7

1-800-663-7639, 24 hours a day, seven days a week
infocanada@insight.org

Australia:

Insight for Living, Inc.
20 Albert Street
Blackburn, VIC 3130, Australia

Toll-free 1800 772 888 or (03) 9877-4277, 8:30 A.M. to 5:00 P.M., Monday to Friday

World Wide Web:

www.insight.org

Study Guide Subscription Program

Study guide subscriptions are available. Please call or write the office nearest you to find out how you can receive our study guides on a regular basis.